EARLY BIRD
PHYSICS BOOKS

SCREWS

by Sally M. Walker and Roseann Feldmann
photographs by Andy King

Lerner Publications Company • Minneapolis

For my daughter, Chrissie, love you forever—RF

The publisher wishes to thank the Minneapolis Kids program for its help in the preparation of this book.

Additional photographs are reproduced with permission from: © Jeff Greenberg/Visuals Unlimited, p. 10; © C. Lee/PhotoDisc, p. 11; © Steve Callahan/Visuals Unlimited, p. 12; © Kim Fennema/Visuals Unlimited, pp. 15, 42; © Dan Mahoney/IPS, p. 28; © Carl Weatherly/PhotoDisc, p. 43.

Text copyright © 2002 by Sally M. Walker and Roseann Feldmann
Photographs copyright © 2002 by Andy King

Lerner Publications Company
A division of Lerner Publishing Group
241 First Avenue North
Minneapolis, MN 55401 U.S.A.

Website address: www.lernerbooks.com

Library of Congress Cataloging-in-Publication Data

Walker, Sally M.
  Screws / by Sally M. Walker and Roseann Feldmann ; photographs by Andy King.
     p.   cm. — (Early bird physics books)
  ISBN 0-8225-2222-5 (lib. bdg. : alk. paper)
  1. Screws—Juvenile literature. [1. Screws.] I. Feldmann, Roseann. II. King, Andy, ill.
III. Title. IV. Series.
TJ1338.W35 2002
621.8'8—dc21   00-010577

Manufactured in the United States of America
1 2 3 4 5 6 – JR – 07 06 05 04 03 02

CONTENTS

BE A WORD DETECTIVE

Can you find these words as you read about screws?
Be a detective and try to figure out what they mean.
You can turn to the glossary on page 46 for help.

complicated machines   **simple machines**
force   **thread**
screw   **work**

You do work when you sharpen a pencil. Are you working when you play or eat?

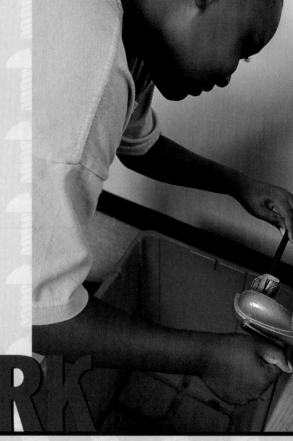

Chapter 1

WORK

You work every day. At home, you work in the kitchen. At school, you sharpen pencils.

It may surprise you to learn that you also work during recess and at lunch. Playing and eating are work, too!

When scientists use the word "work," they don't mean the opposite of play. Work is using a force to move an object from one place to another. Force is a push or a pull. You use force to do chores, to play, and to eat.

These children are using force to climb to the top of a fort.

Sometimes you push or pull an object to move it to a new place. Then you have done work. The distance that the object moves may be long or short. But the object must move. Opening a jar of peanut butter is work. Your force moves the lid.

This girl has used force to open the lid of a jar. She has done work.

Here the girl is using a lot of force to try to turn a lid. But the lid is not moving. Is the girl doing work?

Some lids are too hard to open. You have done no work if you cannot turn the lid. It's not work even if you try until your wrist feels like rubber. No matter how hard you try, you have done no work. The lid has not moved.

An electric drill has many moving parts. What do we call a machine that has many moving parts?

Chapter 2

MACHINES

Most people want to make doing work easy. Machines are tools that make work easier. Some of them make work go faster, too.

Some machines have many moving parts. We call them complicated machines. It may be hard to understand how complicated machines work. Electric drills and clothes washers are complicated machines.

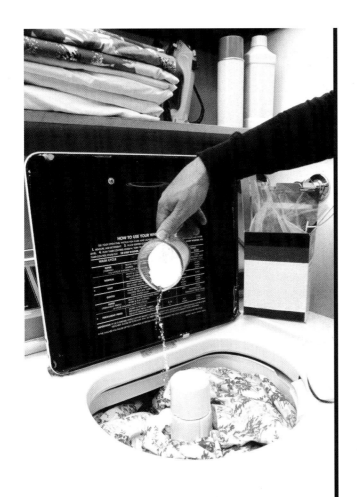

A clothes washer is a complicated machine.

Some machines are easy to understand. They are called simple machines. Simple machines have few moving parts.

A ramp is a simple machine. It has no moving parts.

Simple machines are found in every home, school, and playground. They are so simple that most people don't realize they are machines.

This girl is turning a wheel. A wheel is a simple machine.

A screw is a simple machine that looks much like a nail. What is the difference between a nail and a screw?

Chapter 3

WHAT IS A SCREW?

A screw is a simple machine. A screw looks like a nail with ridges. The ridges on a screw are called a thread.

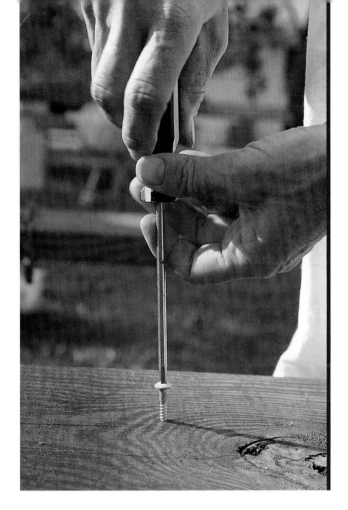

A screwdriver is used to turn a screw into a piece of wood.

A hammer pushes a nail into wood. Your fingers push a pin into fabric. But you don't push a screw. Instead, a screw is turned. The thread on a screw pulls the screw into the material. The material can be wood or metal. It can be Styrofoam or plastic. It can even be concrete or dirt!

A screw seems to have many threads. But it really has just one thread. You can prove this. You will need a sheet of paper, a ruler, a pencil, a crayon or marker, tape, and scissors.

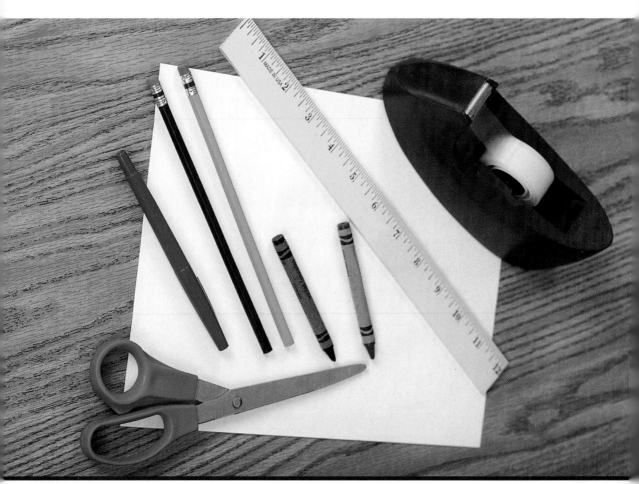

You can prove that a screw has only one thread.
Here are the things you will need.

Use a ruler to measure 3 inches from one corner of your piece of paper.

Make a dot at one corner of the paper. Measure 3 inches from the dot along one edge of the paper. Make an X. Next, measure 3 inches from the first dot along the other edge of the paper. Make another X.

Your line should look like this when you connect the two marks.

Connect the two marks by using a colorful crayon or marker and the edge of the ruler. Your line will be slanted.

Be sure to cut outside the line you have made.

Use the scissors to cut just outside the line.
You will have a triangle with one slanted edge
that is colored.

🔩 *Ask a friend to help you wrap the triangle around the pencil.*

Tape one plain edge of the triangle to the pencil. Make sure you can see the colored line. Next, wrap the triangle tightly around the pencil. Tape the end so the paper will not unroll.

20

Look at your homemade screw. The colored slanted edge is the thread on your screw. The one colorful line looks like three lines wrapped around the pencil. You know there is only one thread. But it looks like more than one thread.

Your screw looks like it has several threads.
But you know it has just one thread.

*How many threads
does the neck of this
jar have?*

Chapter 4

HOW SCREWS HELP US

The neck of a jar has a thread. You can trace the thread from top to bottom. You do not have to lift your finger. So you know that the neck has just one thread.

The neck of a jar is a screw. The jar's lid turns easily on the screw. The lid fits tightly on the neck of the jar. But screwing on a lid takes longer than pushing on a lid. Why does it take longer to screw on a lid?

The neck of this bottle is a screw. You cannot push the lid onto the bottle. You must turn the lid on the screw.

A jar's thread keeps the lid from coming off.

The thread is the reason it takes longer to screw on a lid. Why would you be willing to work longer? Sometimes working longer means the job will be done better.

You can prove this for yourself. You will need a Styrofoam plate and scissors. You will also need a nail and a screw.

🔩 *Sometimes a screw lets you do your work better. You can prove it using these objects.*

Cut the plate into two pieces. Stack one piece on top of the other. Push the nail through both pieces. Try to pull the two pieces of Styrofoam apart. It is probably easy.

It is easy to push a nail through two pieces of Styrofoam. But the nail does not hold the two pieces together well.

It takes longer to turn a screw into the Styrofoam than it takes to push a nail in. But the screw holds the pieces together better.

Stack the two pieces again. This time, turn the screw through both pieces. Try to pull the two pieces apart. It's hard to do. The thread on the screw keeps the screw tightly in place. The pieces of Styrofoam do not pull apart.

The neck of some plastic jugs has a thread. If the jug is dropped, the thread holds the lid tightly in place. So the liquid stays in the jug.

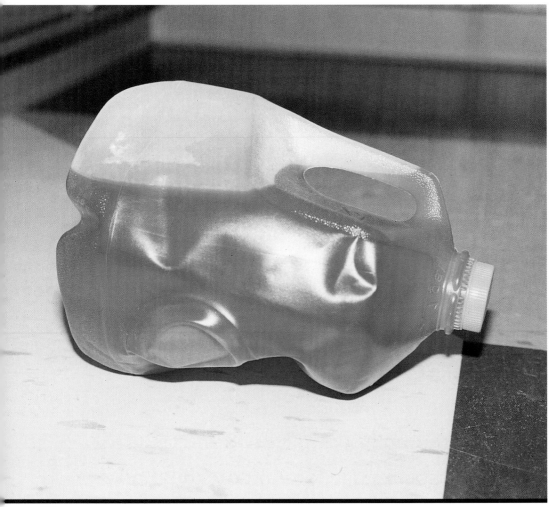

🔩 *The lid of this jug was screwed on. It did not pop off when the jug was dropped.*

 *This jug has a lid that was pushed on. The lid popped off when the jug was dropped.*

The neck of other jugs has no thread. Their lid is pushed on. The lid can pop off if the jug is dropped. Which kind of jug would you rather have fall onto your kitchen floor?

What kind of fastener holds this hinge in place?

Open a door. Look at the hinges that hold the door in its frame. Do you see nails, or do you see screws? A nail's head is smooth. A screw's head has cuts in it. You will see that screws are used on the door's hinges.

Screws keep a door's hinges tightly in place. A door is opened and closed a lot. It would be terrible if hinges pulled out easily. A falling door would hurt people!

A door is opened and closed often. Screws keep it from falling out of its frame.

What is the difference between these two screws?

Chapter 5

KINDS OF SCREWS

Look at several different screws. How are they the same? How are they different? Count the number of thread lines on each screw. Some screws have more thread lines than others. How can you get more thread lines on a screw? You can get more thread lines by changing how steeply the thread slants.

🔩 *You will need to cut a new triangle to make another homemade screw.*

Let's make a new triangle. Make a dot on a different corner of the paper you have already used. Measure 3 inches from the dot along one edge. Make an X. Then measure 6 inches along the other edge. Make an X. Connect the marks by drawing a straight line. Cut out the triangle the same way you did before.

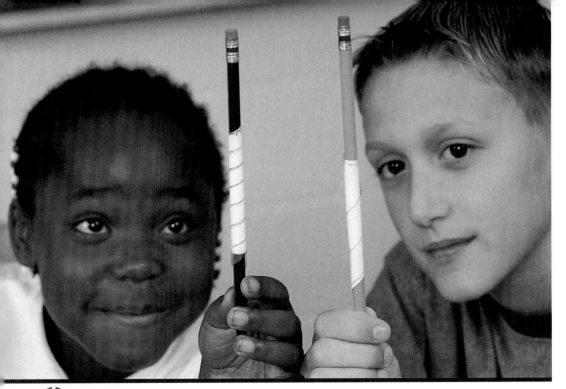

🔩 *One of these screws has more thread lines than the other.*

Next, tape the 3-inch side of this triangle to a pencil. Wrap the triangle around the pencil, and tape the end so that it doesn't unroll. Place your two homemade screws next to each other. Look at the thread lines formed by the new, longer slanted line. Does it look as though there are more lines on this pencil? How many more lines are there?

If a screw has few thread lines, its thread will cut into a material quickly and deeply. You don't have to turn the screw many times to tighten it. But it takes a lot of force to turn it.

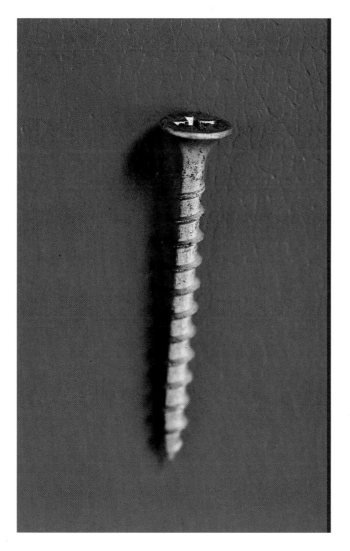

A screw with few thread lines needs to be turned only a few times to tighten it.

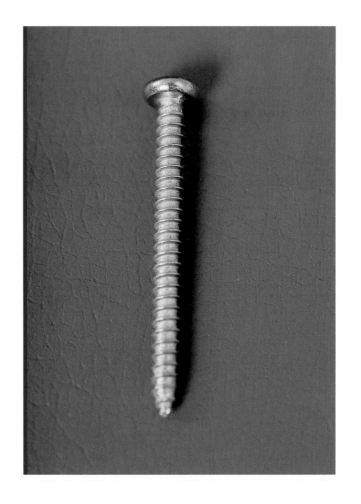

A screw with many thread lines needs to be turned many times to tighten it.

If a screw has a lot of thread lines, its thread will not dig into the material as quickly or as deeply. You have to turn this screw more times to tighten it. But it is easier to turn it. Why is it easier to turn a screw that has more thread lines? Let's find out.

Think about the two triangles you made. The triangle with the short, steep slant made only a few thread lines on your pencil. The triangle with the longer slant made more thread lines on your pencil.

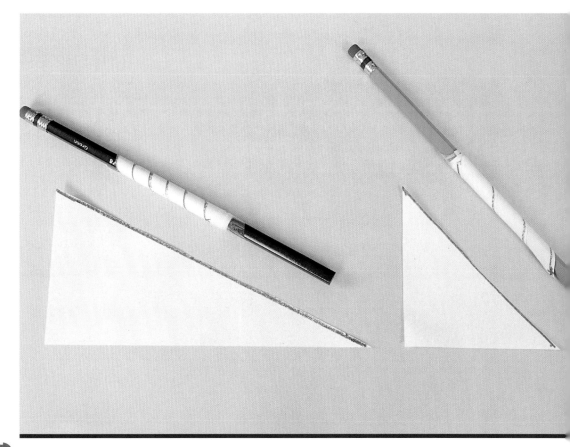

Triangles like these made these two different screws. Which triangle made the screw with more thread lines?

Imagine that your triangles are two hills. It would be hard to climb the short, steep slope. Each step would take a lot of force. It would be easier to climb the longer slope. The longer slope is not as steep. You would walk a longer distance to reach the top. But each step would take only a little force.

HOW A SCREW'S THREAD IS LIKE A SLOPE

Each turn of a screw with few thread lines takes A LOT OF FORCE, just as each step up a short, steep slope takes A LOT OF FORCE.

Turning a screw with only a few thread lines is like climbing a steep hill. Each turn takes a lot of force. Turning a screw with many thread lines is like walking up a longer slope. The screw has to be turned more times. But each turn takes less force. That makes your work easier.

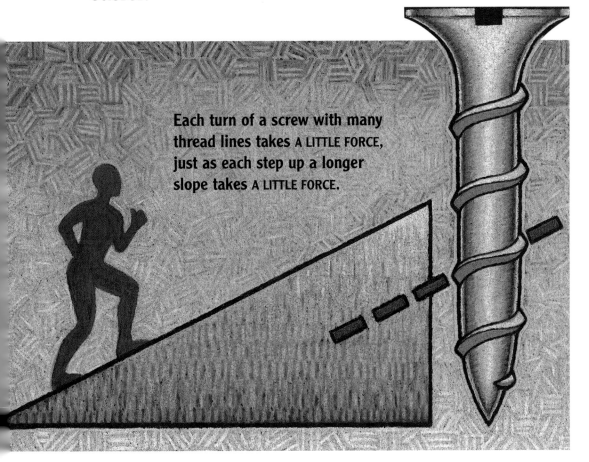

Each turn of a screw with many thread lines takes A LITTLE FORCE, just as each step up a longer slope takes A LITTLE FORCE.

This girl is turning a screw with few thread lines. So she is using a lot of force.

When you turn a screw with few thread lines, the thread digs quickly and deeply. It only takes a few turns to get the screw all the way in. But you must use a lot of force. Using a screw with few thread lines is like walking up a steep hill. It takes fewer steps to get to the top. But the climber uses a lot of force.

40

When you turn a screw with many thread lines, the thread moves just a little deeper with each turn. That means you have to turn the screw more times to get it all the way in. But you use less force. Using a screw with many thread lines is like walking up a gently sloping hill. It takes more steps to get to the top. But the climber uses much less force.

Some people would rather use a screw with many thread lines. Then they can use less force.

You have learned a lot about screws. Using this simple machine gives you an advantage. An advantage is a better chance of finishing your work. Using a screw is almost like having a helper. And that's a real advantage.

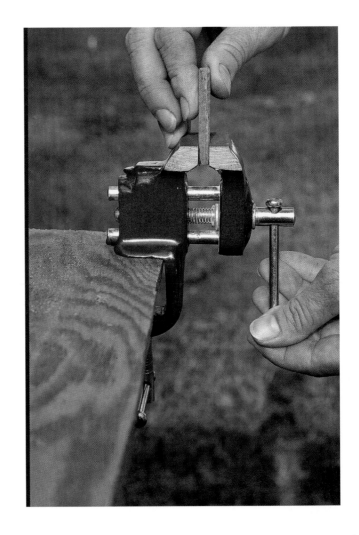

Screws are used in many ways. The screw in this vise helps to hold an object in place.

Simple machines help you when you work and when you play!

ON SHARING A BOOK

When you share a book with a child, you show that reading is important. To get the most out of the experience, read in a comfortable, quiet place. Turn off the television and limit other distractions, such as telephone calls. Be prepared to start slowly. Take turns reading parts of this book. Stop occasionally and discuss what you're reading. Talk about the photographs. If the child begins to lose interest, stop reading. When you pick up the book again, revisit the parts you have already read.

Be a Vocabulary Detective

The word list on page 5 contains words that are important in understanding the topic of this book. Be word detectives and search for the words as you read the book together. Talk about what the words mean and how they are used in the sentence. Do any of these words have more than one meaning? You will find the words defined in a glossary on page 46.

What about Questions?

Use questions to make sure the child understands the information in this book. Here are some suggestions:

> What did this paragraph tell us? What does this picture show? What do you think we'll learn about next? What does it mean to do work? What is a simple machine? Do simple machines make work easier? Why/Why not? Is a screw a simple machine? What are some examples of screws? Can you find this simple machine in your classroom or at home? What is your favorite part of the book? Why?

If the child has questions, don't hesitate to respond with questions of your own, such as: What do *you* think? Why? What is it that you don't know? If the child can't remember certain facts, turn to the index.

Introducing the Index

The index helps readers find information without searching through the whole book. Turn to the index on page 47. Choose an entry such as *thread* and ask the child to use the index to find out if a screw has more than one thread. Repeat with as many entries as you like. Ask the child to point out the differences between an index and a glossary. (The index helps readers find information, while the glossary tells readers what words mean.)

LEARN MORE ABOUT
SIMPLE MACHINES

Books

Baker, Wendy, and Andrew Haslam. *Machines*. New York: Two-Can Publishing Ltd., 1993. This book offers many fun educational activities that explore simple machines.

Burnie, David. *Machines: How They Work*. New York: Dorling Kindersley, 1994. Beginning with descriptions of simple machines, Burnie explores complicated machines and how they work.

Hodge, Deborah. *Simple Machines*. Toronto: Kids Can Press Ltd., 1998. This collection of experiments shows readers how to build their own simple machines using household items.

Van Cleave, Janice. *Janice Van Cleave's Machines: Mind-boggling Experiments You Can Turn into Science Fair Projects*. New York: John Wiley & Sons, Inc., 1993. Van Cleave encourages readers to use experiments to explore how simple machines make doing work easier.

Ward, Alan. *Machines at Work*. New York: Franklin Watts, 1993. This book describes simple machines and introduces the concept of compound machines. Many helpful experiments are included.

Woods, Michael, and Mary B. Woods. *Ancient Machines*. Minneapolis: Runestone Press, 2000. Through photographs and in-depth explanation, this book explores the invention of all six simple machines by various ancient civilizations. It also shows how these machines are the basis of all complicated machines.

Websites

Simple Machines
<http://sln.fi.edu/qa97/spotlight3/spotlight3.html> With brief information about all six simple machines, this site provides helpful links related to each and features experiments for some of them.

Simple Machines—Basic Quiz
<http://www.quia.com/tq/101964.html> This challenging interactive quiz allows budding physicists to test their knowledge of work and simple machines.

GLOSSARY

complicated machines: machines that have many moving parts. Clothes washers and electric drills are complicated machines.

force: a push or a pull. You use force to do chores, to play, and to eat.

screw: a simple machine that looks like a nail with ridges on it. The lids of some jars are also screws.

simple machines: machines that have few moving parts. A screw is a simple machine.

thread: the ridges on a screw

work: using force to move an object from one place to another

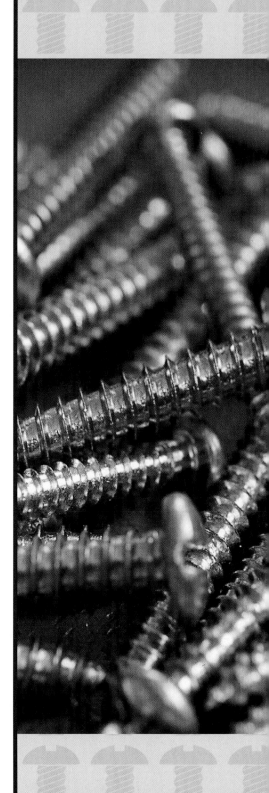

INDEX

About the Authors

Sally M. Walker is the author of many books for young readers. When she isn't busy writing and doing research for books, Ms. Walker works as a children's literature consultant. She has taught children's literature at Northern Illinois University and has given presentations at many reading conferences. She lives in Illinois with her husband and two children.

Roseann Feldmann earned her B.A. degree in biology, chemistry, and education at the College of St. Francis and her M.S. in education from Northern Illinois University. As an educator, she has been a classroom teacher, college instructor, curriculum author, and administrator. She currently lives on six tree-filled acres in Illinois with her husband and two children.

About the Photographer

Freelance photographer Andy King lives in St. Paul, Minnesota, with his wife and daughter. Andy has done editorial photography, including several works for Lerner Publishing Group. Andy has also done commercial photography. In his free time, he plays basketball, rides his mountain bike, and takes pictures of his daughter.

METRIC CONVERSIONS

WHEN YOU KNOW:	MULTIPLY BY:	TO FIND:
miles	1.609	kilometers
feet	0.3048	meters
inches	2.54	centimeters
gallons	3.787	liters
tons	0.907	metric tons
pounds	0.454	kilograms